AF228773

Read for a
Better World™

VOTING AND ELECTIONS

A First Look

PERCY LEED

GRL Consultant, Diane Craig, Certified Literacy Specialist

Lerner Publications ◆ Minneapolis

Educator Toolbox

Reading books is a great way for kids to express what they're interested in. Before reading this title, ask the reader these questions:

What do you think this book is about? Look at the cover for clues.

What do you already know about voting and elections?

What do you want to learn about voting and elections?

Let's Read Together

Encourage the reader to use the pictures to understand the text.

Point out when the reader successfully sounds out a word.

Praise the reader for recognizing sight words such as *a* and *we*.

TABLE OF CONTENTS

Voting and Elections

It's time to vote!

VOTE
TODAY

When we vote,
we make choices.
We can vote for
many things.

We can vote on what
to name our class pet.

8

We can vote on what
game to play.

9

VOTE

We can vote for a leader.
We vote for leaders
in an election.

Leaders talk to voters.

They tell voters
what they will do.

How would you choose
who to vote for?

We choose who
will do the best job.

16

We vote on paper.
People count the votes.

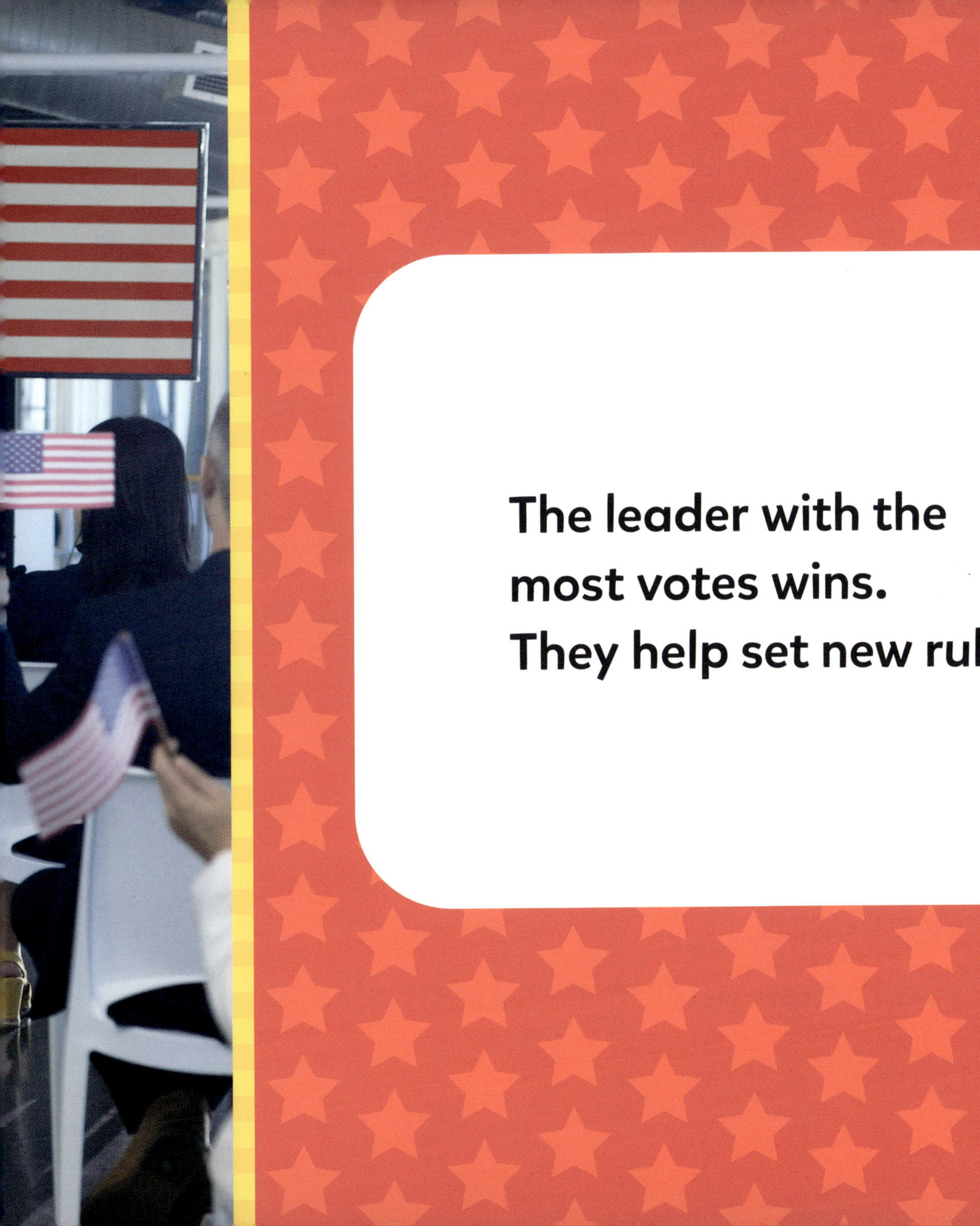

The leader with the
most votes wins.
They help set new rules.

We voted.
We made our voices heard!

You Connect!

What is something you like about voting?

How can you be a good voter?

Why do you think voting is important?

Social and Emotional Snapshot

Student voice is crucial to building reader confidence. Ask the reader:

What is your favorite part of this book?

What is something you learned from this book?

Did this book remind you of any elections you or your family have voted in?

Photo Glossary

Learn More

Farrell, Kate. *V is for Voting*. New York: Henry Holt Books for Young Readers, 2020.

Shulman, Mark. *I Voted: Making a Choice Makes a Difference*. New York: Holiday House, 2020.

Wing, Natasha. *The Night Before Election Day*. New York: Grosset & Dunlap, 2020.

Index

Photo Acknowledgments

The images in this book are used with the permission of: © cglade/iStockphoto, pp. 4–5; © Rawpixel.com/Shutterstock Images, pp. 6–7, 9; © KPG-Payless2/Shutterstock Images, pp. 8, 23; © adamkaz/iStockphoto, pp. 10–11, 23; © SDI Productions/iStockphoto, pp. 11–12, 23; © Pressmaster/Shutterstock Images, p. 13; © pressmaster/Adobe Stock, pp. 14–15; © iammotos/Adobe Stock, pp. 16, 23; © richjem/iStockphoto, p. 17; © wavebreak3/Adobe Stock, pp. 18–19; © CHRISTINE GLADE/Adobe Stock, p. 20.

Cover Photograph: © 5D Media/Shutterstock Images

Design Elements: © Mighty Media, Inc.

Copyright © 2024 by Lerner Publishing Group, Inc.

All rights reserved. International copyright secured. No part of this book may be reproduced, stored in a retrieval system, or transmitted in any form or by any means—electronic, mechanical, photocopying, recording, or otherwise—without the prior written permission of Lerner Publishing Group, Inc., except for the inclusion of brief quotations in an acknowledged review.

Lerner Publications Company
An imprint of Lerner Publishing Group, Inc.
241 First Avenue North
Minneapolis, MN 55401 USA

For reading levels and more information, look up this title at www.lernerbooks.com.

Main body text set in Mikado a Medium.
Typeface provided by Hannes von Doehren.

Library of Congress Cataloging-in-Publication Data

Names: Leed, Percy, 1968–author.
Title: Voting and elections : a first look / Percy Leed.
Description: Minneapolis : Lerner Publications, 2024. | Series: Read for a better world. Read about citizenship | Includes bibliographical references and index. | Audience: Ages 5–8 | Audience: Grades K–1 | Summary: "As citizens we get to choose who our leaders are. We also get to help set the rules. Leveled text and full-color photographs encourage young readers to learn more about elections"—Provided by publisher.
Identifiers: LCCN 2023011297 (print) | LCCN 2023011298 (ebook) | ISBN 9798765608760 (library binding) | ISBN 9798765624647 (paperback) | ISBN 9798765616666 (epub)
Subjects: LCSH: Voting—United States—Juvenile literature. | Elections—United States—Juvenile literature.
Classification: LCC JK1978 .L43 2024 (print) | LCC JK1978 (ebook) | DDC 324.60973—dc23/eng/20230316

LC record available at https://lccn.loc.gov/2023011297
LC ebook record available at https://lccn.loc.gov/2023011298

Manufactured in the United States of America
1 – CG – 12/15/23